D0845986

БЛОКНАЯ
БЛ8IB Л.

EDGE
BOOKS

# THE KIDS' GUIDE TO

# CLASSIC

# games

by Sheri Bell-Rehwoldt

Capstone
press®

Mankato, Minnesota

M MEMORIAL LIBRARY
AINT, MN 55021

Edge Books are published by Capstone Press,
151 Good Counsel Drive, P.O. Box 669, Mankato, Minnesota 56002.
www.capstonepress.com

Copyright © 2009 by Capstone Press, a Capstone Publishers company.
All rights reserved. No part of this publication may be reproduced in whole or in
part, or stored in a retrieval system, or transmitted in any form or by any means,
electronic, mechanical, photocopying, recording, or otherwise, without written
permission of the publisher.
For information regarding permission, write to Capstone Press,
151 Good Counsel Drive, P.O. Box 669, Dept. R, Mankato, Minnesota 56002.
Printed in the United States of America

Library of Congress Cataloging-in-Publication Data
Bell-Rehwoldt, Sheri.
    The kids' guide to classic games / by Sheri Bell-Rehwoldt.
    p. cm. — (Edge books. Kids' guides)
    Includes bibliographical references and index.
    Summary: "Provides instructions and rules for classic indoor and outdoor
children's games" —Provided by the publisher.
    ISBN-13: 978-1-4296-2273-8 (hardcover)
    ISBN-10: 1-4296-2273-3 (hardcover)
    1. Games — Juvenile literature. I. Title.
 GV1203.B543 2009
 790.1'922 — dc22                                        2008029686

**Editorial Credits**
Christopher L. Harbo, editor; Bobbi J. Wyss, designer;
    Marcy Morin, project production

**Photo Credits**
Capstone Press/Karon Dubke, cover, 1, 10
Capstone Press/TJ Thoraldson Digital Photography, all other interior photos

1 2 3 4 5 6 14 13 12 11 10 09

# Table of Contents

Admit it. You love playing games. When your parents were kids, they probably loved playing games too. In fact, they might have spent all of their free time playing games with their friends.

Yes, that was a long time ago. But don't call your parents "old!" Call them "classic," just like the games in this book. Many of the games in this book are still played around the world. Why? Because they're fun! And today is your chance to play them too!

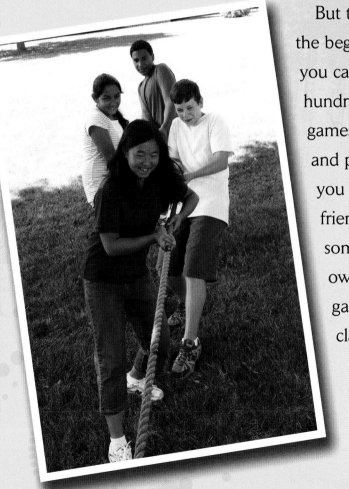

But these games are just the beginning of the fun you can have. There are hundreds of great classic games to be discovered and played. See how many you can play with your friends. Then think up some new games of your own. Someday your games might be classics too!

# BOX IT UP

## What You Need

* ★ pencils
* ★ paper
* ★ 2 players

Your grandparents probably played this old paper and pencil game. If they're not around to play, grab a friend. The player who forms the most boxes by connecting the dots wins!

**Step 1:** Use a pencil to draw a grid of 36 small dots on your paper, as shown.

**Step 2:** Ask your opponent to draw a line between two dots. This line can be **horizontal** or **vertical**.

« **horizontal** flat and parallel to the ground »
« **vertical** straight up and down »

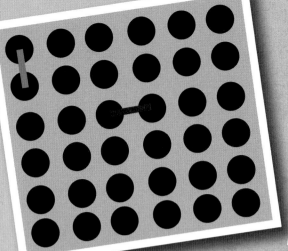

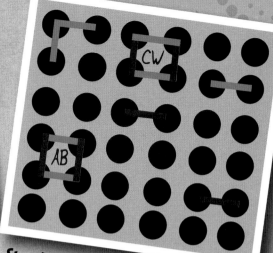

**Step 3:** Now draw your own line between two dots. Continue taking turns.

**Step 4:** At first you'll be able to draw lines far from your opponent's. But soon the lines will begin forming boxes. When your opponent draws the third line of a box, your goal is to add the fourth line to complete it. Your opponent has the same goal.

**Step 5:** Put your initials in each box you complete. Your opponent should do the same.

**Step 6:** Each time you complete a box, you take another turn. Your turn ends only when your last line doesn't complete a box.

**Step 7:** When all the dots are connected, count the number of boxes each player claimed. The player with the most boxes wins.

7

F ★☆☆

# PIPELINE

## What You Need

* pencil
* paper
* red marker

* blue marker
* 2 players

Like Box It Up, this paper and pencil game uses dots. But this game is a lot harder. To win, a player has to draw one long line all the way across the board.

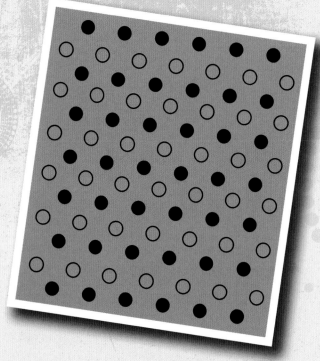

**Step 1:** Use a pencil to draw 13 horizontal rows of dots and circles on your paper, as shown.

**Step 2:** Let your opponent choose either the dots or the circles. If she chooses circles, she may only connect the circles. Then you may only connect the dots.

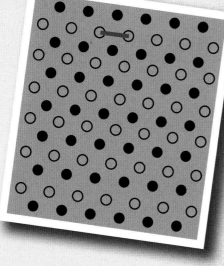

**Step 3:** Let your opponent choose a marker. She starts the game by drawing a line between two of her circles. The line can be horizontal or vertical. Her goal is to win by drawing a **continuous** line across her seven rows. Your goal is to draw a continuous line across your seven rows.

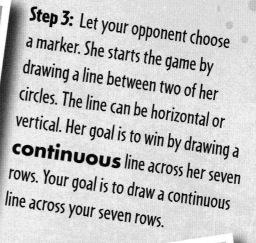

**Step 4:** On your turn, use your marker to draw a line. You can begin far from your opponent's line. Or you can block her line by drawing a line in front of hers. Players may not draw a line through another line.

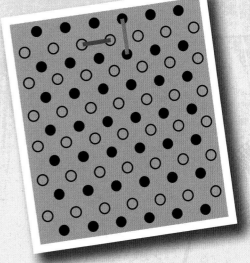

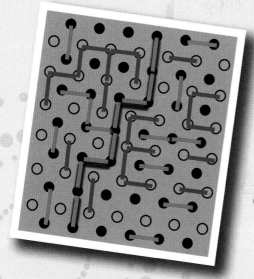

**Step 5:** If you blocked her, she must start a new line on her turn. If you didn't block her line, she could decide to block yours. The winner is the first person to draw a continuous line across seven rows.

« **continuous** when something does not stop »

# SPIDERWEB

## What You Need

★ 20-foot (6-meter) piece of string for each player   ★ 4 or more players

**Step 1:** Decide where to play. A large living room or a backyard works well. Loosely tie one end of each string to a single object, such as a chair.

This game is a lot of fun because it's usually played at warp speed. To anybody watching, the players look like high-speed spiders!

**Step 2:** Wind each string around and through nearby objects. If you're playing outside, a car, deck furniture, and bush branches work well. Inside, use furniture, stair rails, and even potted plants.

**Step 3:** When you've reached the end of each string, firmly tie it to another object. The strings can be tied to different objects. When you're done, the strings should crisscross each other like a spiderweb. You've just created a big obstacle course for the players.

**Step 4:** Gather the players at the starting point. Untie the strings and hand one to each player. When you yell "Go!" everyone must follow their strings. They must free the strings from obstacles as they go. The first player to wind up his string neatly and reach its tied end wins.

# ROCK, PAPER, SCISSORS

## What You Need

★ **2 players**

This game is as "old as the hills," which means it's been around forever! It remains popular because you only use your hands. It can be played anytime, anywhere.

**Step 1:** Show the other player the game's three hand gestures. They are:

Paper: Hold your hand out flat with your palm down.

Rock: Make your hand into a fist.

Scissors: Make a fist, but extend your first and second fingers out in a "V" shape.

GAME CONTINUED ON PAGE 12 ▶▶▶

**Step 2:** Make sure the players agree on the rules. Rock wins over scissors because rock smashes scissors. Scissors wins over paper because a scissors cuts paper. Paper wins over rock because paper wraps around rock.

**Step 3:** Players start the game by tapping their fists three times on their open palms. On the third tap, each player gestures with rock, paper, or scissors.

**Step 4:** If the gestures are different, determine who wins based on the rules above. If the players pick the same gesture, it's a tie.

**Step 5:** The winner is the player who leads after 10 **rounds**.

« **round** a period of play in a sport or contest »

# ULTIMATE DISC TOSS

## What You Need

* large rectangular grassy area
* 4 plastic cones
* coin
* flying disc
* 8 to 14 players

Who knew a spinning plastic disc would create so many die-hard game fans? Here's your chance to join them on the field.

**Step 1:** Divide the players into two teams. Give each team two cones to mark the end zones and sidelines. Each end zone should be about 100 feet (30 meters) wide. The two end zones should be about 200 feet (60 meters) apart.

**Step 2:** Toss a coin to determine the offensive team. These players have control of the disc first.

**Step 3:** Both teams line up in their end zones. Play begins when a defensive player throws the disc toward the offensive team. The offensive team tries to catch the disc before it hits the ground. When players do, the offensive team runs toward the defensive team's end zone. They toss the disc between one another as they run down the field.

**Step 4:** As in football, the defensive players shadow offensive players. The defensive players try to grab the disc or knock it to the ground before it reaches their end zone. However, players cannot touch each other. Shoving, kicking, and tackling are not allowed.

**Step 5:** The offensive team continues moving the disc up the field by throwing it in any direction to one another. Any player holding the disc must stop and throw the disc within 10 seconds.

13

GAME CONTINUED ON PAGE 14 ▶▶▶

**Step 6:** If the disc hits the ground while being passed, the defensive team gains control of the disc. This is called a turnover. Turnovers also occur when a defensive player catches the disc or the disc goes out of bounds. Turnovers do not stop play. The defensive team becomes the offense if it takes control of the disc. That team then tries to move the disc to its opponent's end zone.

**Step 7:** When players catch the disc in their opponent's end zone, they score a point.

**Step 8:** After a score, the scoring team restarts play the same way the game started in step 3.

**Step 9:** Each team may call four time-outs, two per each half of the game. If the final score is to be nine points, then the halftime break occurs when a team scores five points.

**Step 10:** Play continues until an agreed-upon score is reached.

# RED ROVER

## What You Need

* **2 teams of players, evenly split**

This large group game needs just two teams and a roomy area. A large gym or grassy field works best. Courage and a strong grip help too!

**Step 1:** Divide the group into two teams by having each person count off as a "1" or "2."

**Step 2:** Have the two teams stand about 30 feet (9 meters) apart, facing each other. The players join hands. They are not allowed to lock arms at the elbow.

**Step 3:** The game starts with players from one team deciding which player to call over from the other team. Their goal is to choose a player that will be unable to break through their clasped hands. Let's say the team agrees on Bobby. The team loudly chants, "Red Rover, Red Rover, send Bobby right over." Bobby then runs toward their line. He tries to break the handhold of the two players he thinks have the weakest grip.

15

**Step 4:** If Bobby succeeds at breaking through their hands, he rejoins his team. He also takes one person from the opposing team back with him.

**Step 5:** If Bobby fails to break through the line, he becomes part of the team that called him over.

**Step 6:** Next, Bobby's old team calls over a player from his new team.

**Step 7:** The teams take turns calling each other over. A team wins when it ends up with all of the players.

# OLD MAID

## What You Need

★ **2 to 8 players**          ★ **standard deck of playing cards**

This card game is really fun with a crowd because no one wants to get stuck being the "Old Maid!" Unless you can hand this card off to another player, expect to earn a new nickname.

**Step 1:** Pick one player to be the dealer.

**Step 2:** Have the dealer remove three of the queens from the deck of cards and put them back in the box.

**Step 3:** The dealer then deals out all the cards to the players. If the number of players is uneven, some players will have more cards than others, but that's okay.

**Step 4:** The players look at their cards. They then discard any pairs. They should place the pairs face down in front of them.

**Step 5:** The dealer starts the game. She holds her cards face down like a fan. She offers the cards to the player on her left.

**Step 6:** The player takes one card and looks to see if it matches a card she already has. If so, she places the pair face down on the table.

**Step 7:** This player then fans her cards face down. She offers them to the player on her left.

**Step 8:** Play continues around the circle. Players try to discard any pairs on each turn. If a player discards all of her cards without picking the queen, she is safe. The player left holding the queen, also known as the old maid, earns the nickname "old maid."

# SCULPTOR

Think you've got a poker face? Perfect balance? Prove it here by keeping your pose!

## What You Need

* **5 or more players**

**Step 1:** Choose one player to be the "sculptor."

**Step 2:** Have the sculptor pose each player. The sculptor should not touch the players. Instead, she tells the players how to move their arms, legs, and heads.

**Step 3:** The sculptor's goal is to make one of the players smile, laugh, or break his pose. But the players' goal is to stay stone-faced and absolutely still. The sculptor may change the poses as often as she likes. The more difficult the poses are, the harder it will be for the players to stay focused.

**Step 4:** The first player to "crack" by smiling, laughing, or moving becomes the new sculptor. The game continues until the players get too tired to make more poses.

# COIN COLLECTOR

## What You Need

* **4 or more players**     * **blindfold for each player**     * **15 assorted coins for each player**

**Step 1:** Choose someone to be the judge.

Is it possible to correctly sort coins into piles if you can't use your eyes? Slip on a blindfold and see how you do. Your fingers will have to work overtime as they try to "see" the coins.

**Step 2:** The judge sits the players in a line. Then he makes sure they put their blindfolds on correctly. When satisfied, he tells the players to put their hands in their laps.

**Step 3:** The judge puts 15 coins in front of each player. Then the judge yells, "Go!"

**Step 4:** The players rush to sort the coins into piles by **denomination**. Will they be able to tell a penny from a nickel? If you want to make the game harder, have the players also organize their piles in order from the largest value to the smallest value. Or add in some rarely used coins, like half dollars and dollars.

**Step 5:** When a player thinks he has his piles sorted correctly, he yells, "Stop!"

**Step 6:** The other players immediately put their hands in their laps. If the judge decides the piles are right, the player wins and the game ends. But if he's sorted them wrong, he's disqualified and the judge restarts the game.

« **denomination** a value or unit in a system of measurement, such as money »

# PING-PONG SOCCER

## What You Need

* ★ coffee table
* ★ Ping-Pong ball
* ★ 4 players

Some of your friends probably like to boast about their skills on the playing field. Have them try this game. They might get really winded!

**Step 1:** Have the players divide into two teams. The teams should kneel at opposite ends of the coffee table.

**Step 2:** Play begins with one player dropping the Ping-Pong ball in the center of the table.

**Step 3:** Each team tries to blow the ball off the opposing team's end of the table. Doing so earns the successful team a point!

**Step 4:** If the ball rolls off the sides of the table, neither team scores. Continue the game by repeating step 2.

**Step 5:** Play continues until a set score is reached.

# TUG-OF-WAR

## What You Need

* large outdoor area
* electrical tape
* thick hemp rope, 100 feet (30 meters) in length
* tape measure
* 8 players
* 1 judge

Sometimes you need to know if your friends can pull together in a tough situation. In this game, you'll need some friends with real muscle!

**Step 1:** Find a big grassy area, like your backyard or a park. There should be enough space to pull the ends of the rope tight.

**Step 2:** Lay a long strip of electrical tape on the grass. The teams will stand on opposite sides of this dividing line.

**Step 3:** Unwind the rope. Mark the center of the rope by wrapping a short piece of electrical tape around it.

**Step 4:** Use a tape measure to measure 5 feet (1.5 meters) to the right of the center point. Mark this spot with a long piece of the tape. The tape should hang down about 1 foot (.3 meter) from the rope. This tape is one team's flag.

**Step 5:** Measure 5 feet (1.5 meters) to the left of the center point. Mark the rope as you did in step 4.

**Step 6:** Measure another 2 feet (.6 meter) from each of the marks made in steps 4 and 5. Mark the spots by wrapping short pieces of tape around the rope. These lines mark how closely the teams can stand to the center of the rope.

**Step 7:** Divide the players into two teams. Have the teams grasp opposite ends of the rope. Stagger the members on each team so that there are members on the left and right sides of the rope. This will keep them from tripping over one another.

**Step 8:** Be sure the two heaviest players are last in line.

**Step 9:** To start the game, position the center of the rope directly over the dividing line on the grass.

**Step 10:** When the judge yells "Go!," the two teams pull as hard as they can. The goal is to pull the other team's flag over the dividing line.

# HORSE

## What You Need

* basketball
* basketball hoop

* 2 or more players

This basketball game gives you the chance to show off your awesome shooting skills. Just don't spell the word "horse."

**Step 1:** Grab your basketball and head for a nearby basketball hoop.

**Step 2:** The game starts with the first player shooting the ball from any position he chooses. If he makes a basket, the second player must copy the shot from the same spot on the court. If the second player misses the shot, she gets the "h" from the word "horse."

**Step 3:** If the first player misses, the second player can shoot from any spot on the court. If her shot makes the basket, the first player must copy it.

**Step 4:** Play continues like this until one player gets all the letters in the word "horse" and loses the game.

**Step 5:** For three or more players, each player gets a chance to copy the first player's shot. Anyone who misses the shot gets a letter. Then the second player throws a new shot that must be copied by the other players.

**Step 6:** Play then cycles through all the players, with each getting a chance to make the new shot.

**Step 7:** The first player to spell "horse" loses the game.

# RINGER

## What You Need

* chalk
* smooth play surface
* 1 glass shooter marble per player
* 13 glass marbles
* 2 to 6 players

Marble games are great fun. They were even played by ancient Egyptians. For most people, the fun comes from the satisfying sound they hear when an opponent's orb is knocked out of play!

**Step 1:** Use the chalk to draw a 10-foot (3-meter) **diameter** circle on the ground.

24

**Step 2:** Allow the players some warm-up time. If any are new to shooting a marble, teach them how with these steps:

A. Hold out the hand you write with.

B. Tuck your thumb into your palm.

C. Make a fist, wrapping your fingers around your thumb. Keep your thumb knuckle level with your index finger.

D. Grip the marble between the tip of your index finger and your thumb knuckle.

E. To shoot, flick your thumb hard against the marble. Keep the rest of your hand in a fist.

« **diameter** the length of a straight line through the center of a circle »

**Step 3:** When ready to play, arrange the 13 marbles in a cross in the center of the ring. The easiest way to make the cross is to put one marble in the center. Then add three marbles facing east, west, north, and south.

**Step 4:** Players take turns using their shooter marble to knock any marbles out of the ring. A player's first shot can be anywhere on the edge of the circle. If a player's shooter does not travel more than 10 inches (25 centimeters), the player may call out "Slips!" and shoot again from the same spot.

GAME CONTINUED ON PAGE 26 ▶▶▶

BUCKHAM MEMORIAL LIBRARY
FARIBAULT, MN 55021

**Step 5:** If a player knocks a marble outside the ring, she gets to keep it. She then gets another turn.

Fun Factor: ★★☆        Complexity: ★★★

**Step 6:** If a player's shooter marble is still inside the circle for her second shot, she may place her non-shooting hand inside the circle. That way, she can balance herself on her knuckles. If she steps into the ring, she gives up a marble. Her turn ends if she misses a marble. Her turn also ends if her shooter rolls out of the circle or a marble she hits fails to roll out of the circle.

**Step 7:** If the player's first shot doesn't knock a marble out, her turn ends. If her shooter is still in the ring, she must leave it there until the other players have taken a turn. The other players will likely try to shoot at it. Why? Because a player gets a second shot if she hits another player's shooter marble. In addition, if a player's shooter gets knocked out, she's out of the game. Any marbles she has collected go to the player who knocked her shooter out of the circle.

**Step 8:** If a player's shooter is still in the circle on her next turn, she resumes play with it, as she did in step 6. She must not step into the circle but can balance herself on her knuckles. If her shooter is outside the circle, she shoots from the edge of the circle.

**Step 9:** The game ends when the last marble is shot out of the circle. The player with the most marbles wins the game.

# PAPER FOOTBALL

## What You Need

* notebook paper
* scissors
* rectangular table
* coin
* 2 players

Think you have a steady hand and a sharp eye? Then prove it with this paper version of football!

**Step 1:** Cut your piece of paper in half lengthwise.

**Step 2:** Fold the paper over in half.

**Step 3:** Fold the lower right edge up to the fold edge.

**Step 4:** Fold the triangle until you're left with a rectangle at the end of the paper.

**Step 5:** Fold the top left corner of the rectangle down.

**Step 6:** Tuck the flap into the pocket of the triangle.

27

**GAME CONTINUED ON PAGE 28** ▶▶▶

Fun Fac ★★☆

**Step 7:** Opponents sit on opposite sides of a table. They flip a coin to see who will go first. The winner is the "kicker." The loser is the "receiver."

**Step 8:** The game starts with the kicker resting the football over the edge of the table. He flicks the football with his index finger. His goal is to launch the football and land it close to his opponent's edge of the table. Wherever the football lands is where the receiver begins play. If the ball flies off the table, the receiver places the football in the center of the table. He starts play from there.

**Step 9:** The players then take turns flicking the football back and forth across the table. When a player gets the football to hang over his opponent's edge of the table, he scores a touchdown. Touchdowns are worth six points.

**Step 10:** After scoring a touchdown, the player may try for a 2-point conversion. He places the football in the center of the table. He then flicks the ball. If the football hangs over his opponent's edge of the table, he gets two points.

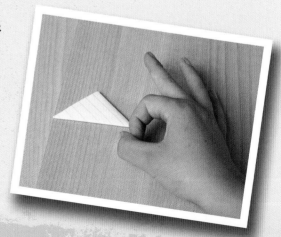

**Step 11:** After a touchdown, a player may try for an extra point instead of a 2-point conversion. An extra point is earned by kicking the football through two goalposts. The opposing player makes the goalposts with his fingers.

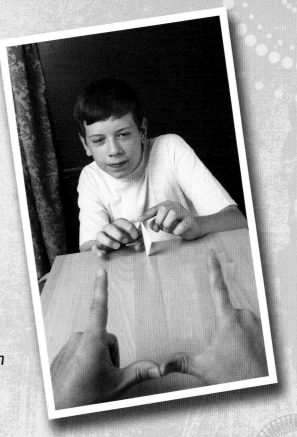

**Step 12:** After a 2-point conversion or an extra point attempt, the opposing player kicks off and regular play resumes.

**Step 13:** If the football flies off the table during regular play, it is out of bounds. The football goes to the opposing player for a kickoff. If either player gets three out of bounds, his opponent can try a field goal. Field goals are kicked the same way as extra points, but they are worth three points.

**Step 14:** The game is played for an agreed amount of time. When time runs out, the player with the highest score wins.

# GLOSSARY

**classic** (KLASS-ik) — of very good quality and likely to remain popular for a long time

**continuous** (kuhn-TIN-yoo-uhss) — when something does not stop

**denomination** (di-nom-uh-NAY-shuhn) — a value or unit in a system of measurement, such as money

**diameter** (dye-AM-uh-tur) — the length of a straight line through the center of a circle

**horizontal** (hor-uh-ZON-tuhl) — flat and parallel to the ground

**opponent** (uh-POH-nuhnt) — a person who competes against another person

**round** (ROUND) — a period of play in a sport or contest

**vertical** (VUR-tuh-kuhl) — straight up and down

30

# READ MORE

**King, Bart.** *The Pocket Guide to Games.* Layton, Utah: Gibbs Smith, 2008.

**Strother, Scott.** *The Adventurous Book of Outdoor Games: Classic Fun for Daring Boys and Girls.* Naperville, Ill.: Sourcebooks, 2008.

# INTERNET SITES

FactHound offers a safe, fun way to find educator-approved Internet sites related to this book.

Here's what you do:

1. Visit *www.facthound.com*
2. Choose your grade level.
3. Begin your search.

This book's ID number is 9781429622738.

FactHound will fetch the best sites for you!

# INDEX

# ABOUT THE AUTHOR

Sheri Bell-Rehwoldt fondly remembers the long summer days of her childhood. She and her neighborhood friends would play Red Rover, Tug-of-War, and marbles until their dads whistled for them to come home.

Sheri is an award-winning author. She has written numerous children's books, including *You Think It's Easy Being the Tooth Fairy?*